SUMMARY

As has North Atlantic Treaty Organization (NATO), the European Union (EU) is adapting to the changing regional and global security environment in the wake of the Cold War. Almost immediately, Europe began to recognize that it could not barricade itself from the world and live off the peace dividend while instability rampaged along its border. The existing European security organizations (Organization for Security Cooperation in Europe [OSCE], Western European Union [WEU]) were ill-suited to deal with the host of new challenges, and as the Balkans conflicts revealed, the European contribution to NATO had fallen woefully behind.

European relevance in the security arena required the EU to develop an expeditionary force capability. After nearly a decade of evolution, the concept of a European expeditionary force developed and formed the centerpiece of the European Security and Defense Policy (ESDP) generated during the 1999 EU Helsinki Summit.

Primarily intended for the Petersberg Tasks humanitarian and rescue, peacekeeping, and use of combat forces in crisis management including peacemaking the expeditionary force shall comprise 50,000 to 60,000 troops, with an additional 140,000 troops in support of extended operations. A 5,000-strong police contingent shall supplement the force by providing crisis management expertise. To wean Europe from the United States, the EU will procure sufficient air- and sealift (and sharing of airframes within the EU under the Air Transport and Air Refuelling Exchange of Services (ATARES) agreement; logistics; Command, Control, Communications, Computers, Information, Surveillance, and Reconnaissance (C4ISR); and combat support to provide it with the capability to deploy the force within 60 days and sustain it for a year.

The headline goal is both ambitious and difficult. Realization of the expeditionary force will require European states to reform or abolish conscription; restructure their forces (modularize) to permit multinational formations; invest significantly in airlift (Airbus A400M) to develop a European Air Transport Command; and, improve sealift and sea power capabilities. Moreover, the EU must increase its precision attack and C4ISR capabilities significantly if it wishes to operate alongside the United States.

The United States can foster the development of the ESDP expeditionary force by:

- monitoring EU progress as it develops a light, expeditionary force;

- encouraging modularization of European units;

- encouraging NATO to cover shortfalls in areas such as supression of enemy air defenses (SEAD), sealift, and airlift;

- encouraging NATO to conduct structural reforms to enable it to conduct multiple contingency operations;

- remaining patient, as EU reforms will be slow;

- considering adoption of the ATARES model for increased capability sharing;

- offering the EU the C-17 should the Airbus A400M fail;

- offering the U.S. Civil Reserve Fleet and Naval Ready Reserve Fleet systems for EU study;

- encouraging the Europeans to explore off-the-shelf technology as a cost saving measure;

- formalizing embarkation and debarkation as part of NATO mission essential task listing;

- encouraging Anglo-Dutch Amphibious Force equivalent for southern Europe;

- encouraging EU development of joint surveillance, target attack radar systems (JSTARS);

- encouraging full implementation of the Helsinki Headline Goals, especially C4ISR, precision attack, and sustainability; and,

- encouraging consortiums within the EU as well as between the EU and the United States.

The establishment of an EU expeditionary force makes sense because it increases burden-sharing and also symbolizes shared risk in between the United States and Europe. Now that Europe is secure, the time is ripe for Europe to take on added security responsibilities.

EUROPEAN ADAPTATION
TO EXPEDITIONARY WARFARE:
IMPLICATIONS FOR THE U.S ARMY

INTRODUCTION

The issue of European defense has been the source of far greater conflict since the end of the Cold War than during it. During the Cold War, Europe was dominated by the confrontation between the superpowers, with virtually all the states of Europe either formally or informally members of one or other alliance. Since 1989 Europe has witnessed significant change   the Soviet Union has collapsed and the Warsaw Treaty Organization (WTO) no longer exists, while the North Atlantic Treaty Organization (NATO) has found itself involved for the first time in the actual application of force in Yugoslavia.

Further afield, the end of the Cold War has brought little respite. The previously reticent attitude of the European powers to the deployment of their military forces outside the NATO region has given way to the commitment of significant military forces in a variety of operations both within and outside Europe. These have included the Gulf War and the subsequent operation to relieve the Kurds in Northern Iraq, peace support operations in Cambodia, humanitarian operations in Somalia, operations throughout the Balkans, with Macedonia looking set to be the next deployment, and the dispatch of British troops to Sierra Leone.

While all this has been going on, there has been a significant battle over the changing security agenda. At one level, the various security organizations within Europe, the Organization for Security and Cooperation in Europe (OSCE), Western European Union (WEU), NATO, and European Union (EU), have all sought to take charge of the security agenda. Initially the OSCE (then the Conference on

1

Security and Cooperation in Europe [CSCE]) was viewed as the favorite with many, particularly in Central and Eastern Europe, viewing NATO as a defunct organization similar to the WTO. However, with the CSCE's failure during the early stages of the breakup of Yugoslavia and the WEU currently folding into the EU, we have been left with two dominant European security organizations   NATO and the EU.

At the same time, the security agenda has been challenged.[1] For example, while President of the European Commission (EC) Jacques Delors concluded:

> [w]e cannot limit our horizons to the new Europe. All around us, naked ambition, lust for power, national uprisings and underdevelopment are combining to create potentially dangerous situations, containing the seeds of destabilization and conflict, aggravated by the proliferation of weapons of mass destruction.
>
> The Community must face this challenge. If it is to be worthy of the European ideal it must square up to the challenges of history and shoulder its share of the political and military responsibilities of our old nations, which have always left their mark on history.[2]

More recently, Britain's current Labour government has sought to set out an internationalist agenda. At a key speech made in Chicago during the celebrations of NATO's 50th anniversary, Prime Minister Tony Blair reinforced this point:

> Twenty years ago we would not have been fighting in Kosovo. The fact that we are engaged is the result of a wide range of changes—the end of the Cold War, changing technology; the spread of democracy. But it is bigger than that. I believe the world has changed in a more fundamental way. Globalization has transformed economies and our working practices. But globalization is not just economic, it is also a political and security phenomenon.[3]

While all this has been going on, there has been significant change to Europe's armed forces. Since 1989 they have invariably been reduced in size, and there has been a slow shift away from conscription in favor of professional forces. They also have begun to be reorientated away from their Cold War threat-based tasking with its emphasis on home defense, towards an expeditionary warfare capability in different forms. However, the progress has generally been slow, and in Kosovo the Europeans found themselves totally dependent upon America for the conduct of the majority of the air campaign.[4] When the Americans subsequently put a limit on their own ground deployment, the Europeans struggled to put sufficient land forces together in time to implement the peace agreement.[5]

Commentating after the conflict, European Commissioner Chris Patten stated:

> The first point is that, frankly, Europe is failing to pull its weight in NATO. The statistics are telling. The European members of NATO spend around 60 percent of what the USA spends on defense, but our capacity to project military force is 10-15 percent of Washington's. With some 2 million in our military forces, we scarcely deploy 2 percent of that number for the Kosovo operation. Three-quarters of the aircraft, four-fifths of the ordnance and most of the intelligence in the former Yugoslavia was provided by the U.S. That makes us weaker allies than we should be. We have to put these defects right.[6]

This view is shared within NATO. The Secretary-General recently summarized the problem thus:

> [T]ough decisions on defense restructuring and defense spending have to be made now. Because unless nations provide the necessary and in some cases missing defense capabilities, the scope for political decision making and action by NATO or the EU would be seriously limited.[7]

The author therefore seeks to examine the reality behind the European rhetoric about force capability and makes

3

recommendations for the U.S. Army. This monograph has been divided into four parts:

First, it will set out six reasons, some new and some old, why European states either singularly, in groups, or collectively will use military force in an expeditionary fashion.

Next, it will examine how the two key security institutions within Europe, the EU and NATO, have adapted to the changing strategic environment and assess their proposed developments.

Then, it will identify trends in Europe's power projection capabilities. This will include an examination of changes in posture, force makeup, and procurement programs.

Finally, it will critically evaluate the extent to which the changes in Europe's defense priorities match the likely threat scenarios and force development plans. Implications for the U.S. Army will then be drawn and recommendations made.

SIX REASONS FOR SENDING THE CAVALRY

Six principal reasons exist why the European states, either individually or collectively, will continue to resort to deploying expeditionary forces. First, Europe contains a number of former colonial powers, each with a long history of using military intervention. A history of colonization has left Britain and France, in particular, with vestiges of their empires which continue to require their support, while others still retain an interest in their former colonies. An example of this occurred in 1991 when the French and Belgians flew troops into the former Belgian colony of Zaire to organize the evacuation of Western nations and help suppress rioting. More recently, the British government felt it necessary to deploy forces to Sierra Leone, initially as part of a Services-led evacuation but later in support of the fledgling democratic government.

4

Second, Europe's dependence upon other states for the supply of essential raw materials including oil has received renewed interest. This led then WEU Secretary-General Willem van Eekelen to argue that the movement of defense policy within Europe towards the protection of its wider interests will result in a greater linking of foreign and defense policy. This would be in line with the Clausewitzian argument of military force becoming the extension of foreign and economic policy.[8] More recently, Britain's *Strategic Defense Review* (SDR) expressly argued that, as a defense review, it was foreign policy-led, and SDR has been seen within Europe as a model for others.[9]

Third, external political pressure for the use of military intervention will continue. The United States historically has called upon its European allies for joint action when its own interests have been involved. The European states have also as individuals been firm supporters of United Nations (U.N.) operations. As the U.N. requirement for such operations remains the requisite force, contributions from Europe are likely to remain. Moreover, Europe has three of the five permanent members of the Security Council Russia, France and the United Kingdom. In the case of the latter two, their continued presence on the Security Council has been linked to their support to U.N. operations.

Fourth, the threat posed by the spread of ballistic missiles and weapons of mass destruction encourages the use of preventative military action. Concern has long been expressed in this area, notably in Britain's 1993 Defense Estimates,[10] although less emphasis has been placed upon the issue of national missile defense than on the option of preemptive action.

Fifth, the ramifications of ethnic unrest in the states bordering Europe have caused growing fear. Since the end of the Cold War, turmoil in the Balkans has led the various states of Europe to deploy a significant number of troops to Bosnia and Kosovo. Europe's experience of World War I has left its leaders with a particular fear of conflict escalation within the region, and the area remains a source of deep-seated rivalry. Moreover, the political unrest that percolates in the North African and Near East regions is a source of concern since they have access to Europe.

Sixth, internal politics increasingly have had an important influence as foreign and domestic policy become more entwined. In particular, domestic public opinion influenced by the media has an important role to play vis-à-vis the humanitarian intervention element within military intervention.[11]

INSTITUTIONAL ADAPTATION

The change in the security environment led the states of Europe to reconsider their security goals. The Cold War emphasis upon consensus within NATO and the WEU was rapidly undermined. This was nowhere more clearly evident than in the approaches of the three principal West European states France, Britain and Germany in 1989 to the future institutional map. France had been unable to affect Alliance policy significantly ever since it had withdrawn from NATO's integrated military structure in 1966.[12] This did not present a problem while policy remained fairly static during the Cold War. However, the events of 1989 required NATO to undergo significant changes in order to survive. The French position meant that their influence on this process of deciding changes in Alliance policy was very limited. Within the WEU, however, the active French involvement allowed them to have a far greater say, particularly as a result of their close relationship with Germany in both the EU and WEU. Thus, during the early 1990s, the French emphasized the role of the WEU as a separate security organization allied to the EU rather than as a pillar of the Anglo-Saxon dominated NATO. Yet France still wished to retain an American military presence in Europe, albeit reduced, as a counter to any German revanchism, and it could, therefore, only afford to downplay the role of NATO rather than seek its abolition altogether.

Britain, by way of contrast, had a significant level of influence within NATO and felt that any shift away from NATO in favor of the WEU could only have an adverse effect upon British interests. Furthermore, the WEU lacked a U.S. presence, and Britain, under successive Prime Ministers, wished to preserve what vestiges of the "special relationship" that remained with the United States. Thus the British called for the full participation of France within NATO, rather than emphasizing the WEU, knowing full well that, of the three principal military posts within the Atlantic Alliance, Britain was guaranteed one and the United States the remaining two.[13] Furthermore, a more independent WEU allied to the EU posed significant internal political problems for the then governing Conservative administration with its deep divisions over Europe.

The German position was ambiguous. On the one hand, it wished to maintain the U.S. presence and involvement in Europe through NATO, while on the other, it wished to promote European integration and the developing special relationship that Chancellor Kohl had with President Mitterrand of France. However, for Germany the question of the reunification with East Germany was a more pressing priority. The remaining members of the WEU were arrayed between the British and French perspectives.

As a result, the early and mid-1990s witnessed a considerable amount of European rivalry for control of the European security agenda. In the immediate aftermath of the end of the Cold War, the various institutions were the main forum for interstate rivalry, which brought these institutions into direct conflict with one another and hence delayed institutional adaptation.

However, since the mid-1990s, this has begun to change. The experience in the Gulf and the early years of the Yugoslav crisis encouraged France, under Chirac, to work with NATO, and there began to be talk of France reentering the integrated military structure. At the same time, Britain, under Major, sought to develop the EU's ability to undertake collective action.[14]

This part of the monograph will not address the management changes directly but instead focus on how NATO and the EU have adapted towards an expeditionary capability. It will be undertaken in two parts: first, through an examination of NATO, and second, via an analysis of the EU (the WEU will be considered under the EU given its absorption by the EU).

NATO.

The need for economic and political reform within the states of Eastern Europe and the Soviet Union tended to preoccupy NATO. Nevertheless, at the July 1990 meeting of the North Atlantic Council (NAC), the *London Declaration* was issued.[15] This was the Alliance's first real statement of intent on how it proposed to provide security in the post-Cold War era. In this declaration the Alliance agreed to extend NATO's remit to the political dimensions of security in recognition of the fact that security and stability are not purely defined in terms of the military balance. More importantly, from a capabilities point of view the Alliance agreed to develop a new military strategy, which moved away from "Forward Defense" towards a more relaxed posture modifying "Flexible Response." This aimed to develop smaller, more mobile multinational forces, with reduced emphasis on nuclear weapons.

In November 1991 the NAC agreed with the Alliance's *New Strategic Concept*. In the accompanying press release, the members agreed that "[T]he challenges we will face in this new Europe cannot be comprehensively addressed by one institution alone, but only in a framework of interlocking institutions tying together the countries of Europe and North America."[16] The new strategic concept acknowledged that the Cold War military confrontation was over, and that the security challenges faced by NATO were now multifaceted and multidirectional in nature.[17]

On the military side, the Defense Planning Committee (attended by all members with the exception of France) approved measures aimed at implementing the new Alliance strategy. Of the three major commands, the Allied Command Channel (ACChan) was eliminated, thus ending Britain's control of one of the three major commands.[18] Two main changes occurred. One was the creation of a standing naval force in the Mediterranean (STANDNAVFORMED) in response to the lessons of the Gulf War about the exposure of NATO's southern flank.[19] Second, and more significantly, was the creation of the Allied Command Europe Rapid Reaction Corps (ARRC) based on a pool of 10 divisions under British command.

The January 1994 summit finally resolved a number of issues, with, for example, agreement to partake in out-of-area peacekeeping operations under U.N. auspices. More importantly, the Combined Joint Task Forces (CJTFs) idea was agreed upon, which presented the WEU with the opportunity of using NATO command, control, and support facilities in operations where it was felt that the WEU would be a more suitable body to act than NATO. This also had useful practical implications in that, where the Americans were less inclined to get involved, the Europeans could still obtain American logistical support in areas where they had no comparable capability. Unfortunately, the idea behind the CJTF concept has never been fully implemented, but it is now accepted that, while it was originally earmarked as a tool of the WEU, the mantle has now passed to the EU.

After the adoption of the CJTF concept, attention within NATO was primarily focused on the enlargement issue and supporting the Dayton agreement. As a result, improvements to NATO's capabilities languished. Finally, with the Kosovo conflict as a backdrop, it was agreed in April 1999 at the Washington Conference to adopt a *New Strategic Concept* and implement the *Defense Capabilities Initiative*

(DCI).[20] The latter sets out targets for Alliance improvements for both Article 5 and Nonarticle 5 operations.

A number of lessons from Kosovo have been drawn within NATO, the majority of which had already been identified in the DCI. One additional lesson drawn by the military staff has been the need to reconsider NATO's existing force structures to support Nonarticle 5 as well as Article 5 operations. Currently, the ARRC is NATO's single deployable corps headquarters with the result that, once this unit is deployed, NATO has no other available corps headquarters to deploy. This was clearly evident when it came to relieve the ARRC in Kosovo.

One suggestion has been to create three Higher Readiness Corps, each supported by two lower readiness corps.[21] The goal of such a structure is two-fold. First, it would enable NATO to undertake up to three simultaneous Nonarticle 5 operations at corps level at any time. Second, it has a built-in rotation structure, thus dealing with the problem of what happens after the initial deployment. While not formally approved as yet, these proposals reflect the ongoing movement in NATO's command structure away from territorial defense towards expeditionary warfare. The major limiting factors in these changes are, first, the absence of France from the integrated military structure; and second, the issue of cost in financial and institutional priorities. Enlargement remains a major issue for NATO.

European Union.

The WEU, rather than the EU, was initially seen as the main forum for a European military capability. The importance and role of the WEU in the post-Cold War world was discussed in December 1990 at the WEU Council of Ministers.[22] The subsequent communiqué highlighted the three areas of contention within the WEU, the resolution of which dogged WEU discussions throughout the period: (1) the role of the WEU with the emergence of political union;

(2) the relationship of the WEU to NATO; and (3) the question of out-of-area activities.[23]

Subsequently, at the EU's Maastricht meeting, the *Treaty on Political Union* was signed which established a Common Foreign and Security Policy (CFSP) and the WEU's relationship to the EU. This aimed "to strengthen the security of the Union and its Member States in all ways"[24] and, in practice, the WEU was seen as the main organization for implementing the military side of security policy with the EU providing the other elements.

The members of the WEU agreed to this and promised to provide the requisite structures and means to carry out the tasks of the EU as the French and Germans had wanted. To facilitate this, it was agreed to move the WEU Council and Secretariat to Brussels in order to be closer to the European Commission and also to the NATO headquarters at Mons. The WEU members also agreed to make military units answerable to the WEU, with many of them also earmarked to NATO (double-hatting).

In June 1992 the WEU Ministerial Council met, and the resulting Petersberg Declaration attempted to tackle some of the practical issues.[25] It defined when the WEU would be used, and these became known as the Petersberg Tasks:

- humanitarian and rescue tasks;

- peacekeeping tasks; and,

- tasks of combat forces in crisis management, including peacemaking.

Despite these steps, only a little progress was made subsequently despite NATO's CJTF concept designed with the WEU primarily in mind.

Developments in EU/WEU defense capabilities continued to founder until the EU's Amsterdam summit in June 1997 where the European leaders agreed to provide a crisis management mechanism for the EU partners.[26] More

11

significantly, the United Kingdom launched the European Defense Initiative at an informal EU summit in October 1998. At the Franco-British meeting at St. Malo in December 1998, they agreed that the EU "must have the capacity for autonomous action, backed by credible military forces, the means to use them, and a readiness to do so, in order to respond to international crises."[27]

However, progress remained slow, and the weaknesses in European capabilities were painfully exposed during the Kosovo conflict. This led to a Franco-British call for a European intervention capability at corps level.[28] The Joint Declaration issued in London in November 1999 by the British and French Governments gave a renewed impetus to the St. Malo Declaration and put concrete proposals forward, which were subsequently endorsed at the EU's Helsinki Summit.[29]

The Helsinki meeting in December 1999 marked an historic breakthrough. It was finally decided to give practical effect to the ambitions of the Amsterdam Treaty and the Cologne European Council Declaration by establishing a European military capability.[30] In summary, the:

> EU Member States committed themselves to concrete goals for capability improvement. They specified the scale of armed forces that they should be able to deploy rapidly, with the right skills and equipment, and able to sustain in a theatre of operations until the military job is done. They agreed by the year 2003 they should have modernised their armed forces so as to be able to draw from a pool of deployable units (15 brigades) to tackle the most demanding crisis management tasks, in operations up to corps level (up to 50,000 to 60,000 personnel, together with appropriate air and naval elements). These forces are to be militarily self-sustaining for at least a year. The EU Member States also agreed to develop collective capability goals in such fields as command and control and strategic transport, to address the specific capability shortfalls identified in the audit of European capability undertaken by the Western European Union.[31]

In reality, Helsinki's goal of 50,000-60,000 troops equals roughly 200,000 with rotation.[32] But more than that, it has necessitated a fundamental rethinking of the EU's role. A number of steps have been taken. Both the Council of Minister's Higher Representative and the European Commission have created crisis centers to help manage operations involving such forces. A Political and Security Committee has been set up to help define policies by developing options,[33] and this has been matched by a Military Staff tasked with providing strategic level but not operational planning to the Council of Ministers.

From a NATO perspective, Deputy Supreme Allied Commander Europe (DSACEUR) and the Supreme Headquarters Allied Powers in Europe (SHAPE) have been identified as primary candidates for Operational Commander and Military Strategic Operational headquarters, and DSACEUR will act as strategic coordinator between EU and NATO in peacetime and force generator during a crisis.[34]

The Helsinki goals require the ability to deploy within 60 days and sustain for a year forces up to corps level by 2003. Such a force is supposed to be self-sufficient with necessary C3I, logistics, combat support, and appropriate air and sea assets.[35] To achieve this, a force catalogue has been developed bearing significant similarities to the DCI.

Moreover, Helsinki included the creation of mechanisms for handling civilian aspects of crisis management.[36] This is an area where the EU has the potential to provide a far greater capability than NATO. According to Chris Patten:

> Our experience with humanitarian aid, election monitoring, police deployment and training, border control, institution building, mine clearance, arms control and destruction, combating illicit trafficking, embargo enforcement and counter terrorism shows how comprehensive the Commission's roles already are.[37]

To support this, EU members have agreed to make 5,000 police officers available by 2003 within 60 days, with 1,000 to go within 30 days.[38]

These goals are ambitious, and it is clearly early in the EU's achievement of such capabilities. The one conceptual area lacking is the types of operation envisaged for such a force. Officially it is supposed to cover the full Petersberg range and to expressly exclude collective security. Two types of EU operations have been suggested: first, those using NATO capabilities and assets; and second, those without recourse to NATO assets and capabilities utilizing an existing national or multinational command.[39] However, few within the EU are able to give any scenarios with any conviction apart from the EU taking over a NATO mission once the warfighting side of things has been complete and the United States no longer wishes to be involved. Moreover, the majority of these initiatives are at the embryonic stage and their subsequent development cannot be predicted.

MILITARY ADAPTATION

Military adaptation to expeditionary warfare, like institutional adaptation, generally has been slow. An official French Minister of Defense analysis of Kosovo follows:

> This conflict illuminated the differences between the military means of the United States and Europe. The United States has developed extremely large military means that are justified by America's world ambition since the end of the Second World War. These gaps also result from the research efforts and armament programs underway since the beginning of the 1980s. . . . Our technological backwardness in certain areas, such as information mastery in real time or stealth, is linked to the lower level of financial means allocated to research (Europe's defense research budget is a third of the U.S. one) rather than to the know-how of European companies. The Kosovo conflict has, moreover, revealed quantitative deficiencies that could affect our ability to sustain an operation of long duration as well as

14

capabilities that were completely lacking (cruise missiles, radar satellite observation systems, offensive jammers, aircraft identification systems).[40]

As the Cold War came to an end, the effects of the world recession had already begun to put increasing pressure on individual European governments to reduce defense budgets prior to the changes brought about by the revolutions in Eastern Europe. Domestic public opinion was well ahead of the political leaders in reacting to events in Eastern Europe and rising unemployment at home. In response, defense budgets throughout Western Europe, and indeed throughout Eastern Europe, began to suffer significant cutbacks in real terms in anticipation of the reductions that would be required with the successful completion of the Conventional Forces in Europe (CFE) process.[41] Politicians from a variety of different persuasions spoke of the "Peace Dividend" that would be available as a consequence of these changes.

With few exceptions, a number of trends have become clear in the defense budgets of the European states. The initial planned reductions were largely overtaken by further cutbacks with the exception of Sweden, France, and Greece.[42] However, even these states have had to make further reductions. Thus in the United Kingdom, the *Options for Change* review was rapidly followed by *Frontline First: The Defense Costs Study*.[43] These reviews have generally been about reducing overall numbers and made token adjustments to force makeup. In effect, change equalled less of the same. Only in the last few years have some of the European states embarked upon a third wave of reviews aimed at fundamentally addressing their requirement to develop an expeditionary capability. In this, the Bosnia and more recently the Kosovo experience has added impetus. Here the Strategic Defense Review (SDR) has been seen as the role model for such third generation reviews.[44] The SDR marked the United Kingdom's formal return to an expeditionary capability and set out a number of force goals.

This part will therefore examine some of the key post-Cold War trends in Europe's military. These are: the professionalization of Europe's military mobility, precision attack, and Command, Control, Communications, Computers, Information, Surveillance, and Reconnaissance (C4ISR). While these do not cover the full range of changes that have taken place, they encompass many of the key areas identified in the DCI, the WEU audit of capabilities, and the EU's catalogue of capability requirements. Moreover, they are key requirements for an expeditionary capability and reflect many of the current dilemmas confronting defense planners.

Professionalization of Europe's Military.

The Cold War confrontation with the Soviet Union had encouraged the various European states to introduce conscription in one form or another. This helped to provide relatively large military forces at low cost. However, as the Cold War came to an end, the Western world was confronted by the Iraqi occupation of Kuwait. In Europe, both the United Kingdom and France led the way in contributing forces. Britain was unusual in that it had abandoned conscription during the 1960s and was thus able to draw upon its regular forces. In contrast, France found it difficult to raise sufficient forces. The use of conscripts outside France, and more generally in a war of choice rather than one of national survival, was difficult, and France was forced to replace rapidly its conscripts with regulars in those units scheduled for deployment to the Gulf. Other countries were to find similar problems in other operations, such as the Italian deployment in support of the U.N. peacekeeping force to Mozambique.

As a result, there has been a general move away from conscript forces towards the maintenance of all-volunteer forces. Such practice has been adopted by such countries as Holland, France, and Belgium. This trend has not been universal, with some states wishing to preserve conscription for cultural, societal, or home defense reasons. Sweden and Norway are good examples of those retaining conscription. Consequently, a number of states have sought a halfway house position, increasing the proportion of professional forces and reducing the number, and often length, of conscriptions. Germany, Italy, and Spain are all good examples of this.

This trend has caused a number of problems. In practice, this means that there is a steadily expanding manpower pool within Europe available for use in expeditionary warfare, even though the overall European military manpower pool is diminishing. As a result, individual European states will be more willing to support initial operations; however, sustaining operations in the long run may be problematic. An extreme example of this would be the British experience of 1999 when the Kosovo peacekeeping mission brought the deployment level of the British armed forces to 47 percent for a brief period.[45] From an EU point of view, it has received commitments of more than 100,000 troops for its on-call corps capability, but it has insufficient troops to provide the requisite rotation if it is required to undertake a long-term task at corps level.

Also within this process of adaptation, there have been increasing moves towards the modularization of units below the divisional level in order to provide building blocks for operations, together with the creation of headquarters units to manage multinational operations.[46] This is good; however, the various states are all doing this differently. In the French case, they have adjusted their army to 51 regiments grouped into 9 brigades. Above the brigade level, four divisional headquarters are available for operations, which can also draw on a pool of divisional assets together with the most appropriate mix of the nine brigades. In contrast, the Germans have earmarked certain brigades for the expeditionary role,[47] while the United Kingdom is implementing a system of brigade rotation to provide various levels of unit availability.

17

These changes have not been without costs, and each of these armed forces has had to reconsider its force makeup, particularly in the areas of logistical and administrative support. These support systems have generally taken far longer to adjust because they have received less priority and because a number of the problems have only emerged with the shift to professional forces. The retention of personnel in the wake of an overall reduction in the number of personnel matched to the financial cost of professional armed forces has also become an issue.

Mobility.

In conjunction with the movement towards professionalization, a steady increase in the emphasis given to mobility has occurred. This is most clearly illustrated by the ARRC and the rows surrounding what is now known as the A400M transport aircraft. But progress has been very slow, and the Kosovo experience, more than any other recent operation, highlighted Europe's inability to deploy ground forces rapidly. General Sir Michael Jackson was only able to deploy nine battalion units on the first day of ground operation, four of which were British (two having arrived in the preceding 96 hours). By the second day, two additional battalions had arrived from France and the United Kingdom.[48]

As a result, there have been moves to improve this situation in three ways. First, have been calls to improve airlift. As part of Helsinki, the EU states agreed to prepare to develop a European Air Transport Command.[49] The main procurement program to support this is the Airbus A400M, which had its memorandum of understanding at the recent Paris air show. This included firm orders for 196 aircraft plus probable options for Italy of 16. This program, if completed, will significantly improve Europe's ability to deploy forces by air. Such a force will provide a significantly enhanced lift capability and facilitate the carriage of some outsized loads. Moreover, since it is a collaborative program, it will mean interoperability is less of a problem, and there is the potential to use this as a larger pool of aircraft under the auspices of the Air Transport Command.[50]

A number of states have also purchased the new generation of Hercules transport aircraft. More significantly, the United Kingdom has leased four C-17s from Boeing for 7 years, pending the delivery of A400Ms into service.[51] The first two of these aircraft have already been delivered and have restored a capability lost with the retirement of the Belfast fleet during the 1970s. The deal is important for it marks a means by which a European state has been able to acquire a capability at an affordable price. There are limitations with such a deal in terms of usage, while the small size of the fleet will pose problems, especially if other European countries seek to rely on the aircraft's availability for their own usage under the auspices of the European Air Transport Command.

At a lower level, the European Air Group has obtained the Air Transport and Air Refuelling Exchange of Services agreement (ATARES), whereby individual European states can effectively hire each other's aircraft. The advantage of this lies in the efficiency savings that fall out of the agreement.[52] A further development along this theme has been a Dutch proposal to contribute to the conversion of the German A310 transport aircraft to the tanker/transport role in return for access to these aircraft.

Second have been improvements in sealift. In terms of amphibious lift capability, the Europeans are in the process of significantly improving their capabilities.[53] The Dutch and Spanish have undertaken a joint program to develop a Landing Pad Dock (LPD), with the Dutch now having one ship in service and a second planned for service from 2007, while the Spanish have built two vessels.[54] The British have also adopted this basic design, with four Bay class auxiliary landing ships ordered to replace the earlier Landing Ship Logistics (LSL).[55] The British have also ordered two larger LPDs to replace their existing aging vessels, and the Albion class vessels are scheduled to enter service in 2003. This will operate in conjunction with the HMS *Ocean*, the helicopter carrier, and provide a significant amphibious lift capability. Italy has also modernized its amphibious forces with the construction of the three San Giorgio vessels.[56] France has begun to address its amphibious requirements with the view that the two extra Foudre vessels should now be 21,000-ton helicopter carriers.[57] These developments will mark a significant improvement in the European force capabilities once they all reach service, but, for the next few years, there will be weaknesses as older ships reach the end of their service lives.

Some improvements to the various Marine forces of Europe have been matched to these improvements. Marine units generally have benefited from the end of the Cold War and the increasing stress placed upon an expeditionary capability. The existing Anglo-Dutch Amphibious Brigade remains committed to its NATO tasks and presumably also will become available to the EU as the WEU winds up. It has received a number of improvements, the latest being the delivery of armored personnel carriers to the United Kingdom's forces to replace their unarmored BV-206s.[58] Spain, France, and Italy have increased their level of cooperation, and the British and French have agreed to increase the collaboration between their respective marines.

Strategic sealift, however, still remains underdeveloped. One of the basic problems lies in national rules governing the transportation of military personnel and equipment. A number of states restrict the transport of their personnel and equipment to state registered and/or national crewed ships. Moreover, there is relatively little peacetime training or planning for the deployment of nonmarine units by sea. The single exception to this has been the United Kingdom's decision to acquire a six-vessel roll-on/roll-off capability through a private finance initiative.[59] Once in service, these vessels will provide a unique capability within Europe, similar in some respects to the U.S. Ready Reserve Fleet.

Third, there are initial moves towards the lightening of units. The British have begun to look at replacing the new Challenger 2 MBT in 25 years with a future rapid effect system weighing less than 20 tons. This would form part of what has become termed the Ground Medium Force, operational from 2025 onwards, similar to current U.S. studies.[60] However, only the United States and Britain, within NATO, are studying a replacement tank.[61] A number of states are looking to replace their existing tracked infantry fighting vehicles with wheeled variants, which will be operational towards the end of this decade. Moreover, France traditionally has maintained a light armoured capability based on wheeled vehicles for operations in its former colonies. This third trend is, therefore, only in its infancy and needs to be developed further.

The other trend has been towards the creation of airmobile forces. The Dutch have created an Air Assault brigade supported by attack and support aircraft, while the British have created the 16th Air Assault Brigade to fulfil a similar role. These forces are supported by an increased attack and support helicopter capability.

Precision Attack.

The Kosovo Campaign also highlighted the general weakness in the Europeans precision attack capabilities. Few members of NATO had this capability, and the majority merely provided air defense aircraft to escort NATO's strike packages. There have been some improvements here, with the British and French committed to the purchase of a significant number of precision-guided munitions such as the Storm Shadow, Brimstone, and Maverick. However, there is a time lag before all these become available, and the remaining members of the EU and NATO still have some way to go even to match the current British and French capability. The campaign was noticeable for the first use of Tomahawk Land Attack Missiles (TLAM) from a British submarine. While the British contribution was limited both by the small number of platforms available[62] (one out of a planned force of ten) and the paucity of its stockpile, its political significance was important.[63] Having more than one state able to contribute a particular capability sometimes allowed NATO to strike targets that it might otherwise have been unable to. The importance of the capability seems to have been recognized by both the French and the British. The latter are undertaking a joint U.S./United Kingdom feasibility study into re-engineering the Tactical Tomahawk to allow for its launch from torpedo tubes.[64] The French have begun studies into equipping their attack submarines with a 500km naval variant of the Storm Shadow air-to-surface missile.[65]

Overall, this remains an area of significant weakness particularly in the short term. Both the DCI and the WEU audit of capabilities have identified this as an area for improvement. One solution to this may be the recognition that, in any EU-led operation, there will simply have to be a greater dependence upon so-called "dumb" munitions.

C4ISR.

Command, Control, Communications, Computers, Information, Surveillance, and Reconnaissance (C4ISR) is probably the weakest area from a European point of view. Prior to Kosovo, the Europeans lacked even the capability to conduct a coordinated air campaign.

There have been a number of improvements. At the lower end of the conflict spectrum both the United Kingdom's Permanent Joint Headquarters and its French equivalent, the Centre Operational Interarmees, have the capability to manage smaller crises, but subordinate headquarters may be a problem. The United Kingdom now is developing a CAOC capability able to deploy and manage a limited air campaign. The French, in contrast, have purchased the relevant equipment but mothballed it, with personnel earmarked from other posts to mobilize it when appropriate. This latter approach clearly has problems when it comes to maintaining expertise.

On the land side, both NATO's ARRC, with its predominantly British headquarters, and the Eurocorps offer the basis for potential headquarters, and both have transitioned through the Balkans in recent years. Nevertheless, given the general weaknesses in this area, the development of the idea of U.S. brigades commanding other nations' divisions has appeal, although there would be political sensitivities.

However, the problem is as much political as it is military. Various European states wish to have their "share" of the command leads and capabilities but few wish to invest seriously in the capabilities. Here the Helsinki Headline Goals may become more important than NATO's DCI as a means of encouraging the requisite resources to be allocated to these tasks. A positive note has been struck by the EU's commitment to using NATO doctrine and approaches to warfighting.

Other contentious issues remain. Kosovo was foremost a battle for the control of information. The weaknesses in the existing European intelligence, surveillance, and reconnaissance capabilities were exposed during the Kosovo conflict. In terms of intelligence, the EU, like NATO, entirely depends upon the information supplied by individual nations. In Kosovo, NATO largely depended upon the United States, and this is likely to continue. The EU is likely to remain in a similar position with the British, in particular, unlikely to want to alter their intelligence relationship with the United States to prioritize the EU.[66] Thus, NATO, the EU, and Europe in general are likely to remain dependent upon the United States.

One obvious area for improvement lies in the provision of an airborne radar for monitoring the land battle (U.S. JSTARS program). The United Kingdom has ordered five

23

ASTOR aircraft for delivery in 2005.[67] However, Britain's European partners are further away from fielding any capability, while the ideas of a NATO force similar to its AEW fleet remain unfulfilled. Germany, France, Italy, the Netherlands, and Spain are going ahead with a demonstrator project scheduled for testing in 2005.[68] A NATO force, or indeed a EU force similar to the existing NATO AWACS force, is the logical way ahead, and this needs to be encouraged if it is going to be achieved.

CONCLUSIONS AND RECOMMENDATIONS

Conclusions.

It would be relatively straightforward to argue that the European expeditionary capability is largely a myth, and progress has been and is likely to remain extremely slow. What is already clear is that there is considerable potential for the Europeans to develop their own expeditionary capability. A number of steps have been taken, and it is important to note the words of David Yost: "In contrast with most of its European allies, the United States has been preparing forces for transoceanic power projection for decades."[69]

During the Cold War, Europe's military forces were in many ways able to act autonomously from one another. For example, NATO's Central Front consisted of a number of national corps all working on separate lines of communication, which in wartime they would retreat along. It is only now, with the shift from territorial defense to expeditionary warfare, that there has been a significant requirement to work together, become inter-operable, and create the ability to project forces. The work undertaken by the European Air Group reflects some of the problems and successes encountered. During the Cold War, individual air bases generally supported a particular nation's aircraft. It has taken time to discover and train to support other states' aircraft and to project that capability into the field but this is being achieved.

The United Kingdom's House of Commons Select Committee on Defense rightly concludes that:

> The political advantages of multinational cooperation include sharing risks, demonstrating collective intent and, by acting in unison in pursuit of a common cause, bringing greater international pressure to bear on an adversary than a single nation would be able to do on its own. The military advantages are that cooperation adds depth (strength in numbers) and breadth (additional capabilities) to a force, as well as providing access to national or regional logistic infrastructures and, in certain circumstances, access to high value information and intelligence.[70]

Both NATO's DCI and the WEU's study of capabilities indicated the same basic weaknesses, and the respective members of NATO and the EU have agreed to remedy these. While there has clearly been movement, a considerable amount of ground to cover remains.

Interoperability remains a key issue. The pace of improvement in U.S. information systems continues to widen the gap still further, and the United States already has been forced to retain some legacy systems. There are a number of potential ways to mitigate the problems, particularly in terms of C4ISR. For example, an increasing use of commercial off-the-shelf systems may facilitate a closing of the gap, but it requires the Europeans to emphasize compatibility as a funding priority. In other areas, the fulfilment of the Defense Trade Security Initiative to streamline export controls at least would allow all the EU and NATO members access to key defense capabilities in the first instance.

Alternatively, the adoption of role specialization would allow individual European states to focus their resources on particular capabilities. Here the ATARES agreement might serve as a model of how this could work. It has already been shown to reduce costs, which allow funds to be spent in other

25

areas. Alternatively, increased recourse to the private sector either at the national level or the EU/NATO level may provide the opportunity to maintain or develop capabilities that would otherwise be unaffordable. The disadvantage of such an approach is that it abrogates the idea of shared risk, and it also increases dependency within the EU and NATO.

Recommendations.

- That the U.S. Army continues to monitor developments by the EU in adapting to expeditionary warfare and see how they evolve. At present, they are at such an embryonic stage they neither present a significant capability nor threat to NATO or U.S. interests.

- That the U.S. Army encourages its European allies to standardize their approach to the modularization of their units. This would to facilitate their interchangeability.

- That the U.S. Army reviews what capabilities it lacks in sufficient number and is unlikely to obtain at the national level, and encourages NATO to develop these as a substitute. Examples here include additional SEAD, sealift, and airlift.

- That the U.S. Army encourages NATO in its structural adaptation so that it can support more than one operation at any one time. The U.S. Army needs to consider its own level of commitment to this.

- That the U.S. Army continues to support the ongoing reform of the EU and NATO. The potential for the reform to slow is considerable within both bureaucracies and individual state agendas.

- That the ATARES model be adopted more widely as a means of efficient capability sharing.

- That the European A400M program is pressed ahead as a matter of urgency, and, if it should fail, recourse to the acquisition of C-17s as an alternative be considered. In the short term, other European states should consider the temporary leasing of C-17s from Boeing in a manner similar to the United Kingdom.

- That the Europeans investigate whether they can create their own version of the U.S. Civil Reserve Air Fleet as a means of supplementing their air transport.

- That the Europeans examine whether the use of privately funded capabilities, such as the United Kingdom's six ALSLs, will provide capabilities at an affordable price.

- That the Europeans reconsider their respective national legislation governing the transport of their own personnel and equipment by sea. Here the EU may serve as the perfect platform for coordinating national legislation. This should be aimed at enabling them to be transported by other NATO/EU partners.

- That the process of loading and unloading army units be practiced regularly.

- That the Europeans consider acquiring their own variant of the U.S. Ready Reserve Force, perhaps under the aegis of the EU.

- That efforts to create a southern equivalent to the Anglo-Dutch Amphibious Force be encouraged.

- That NATO presses ahead with its own JSTARS force similar to the existing NATO AWACS force.

- That the Europeans begin to look more seriously at the future construct of their armies and particularly the ideas of a lighter force.

- That the DCI and Helsinki Headline Goals be implemented in full, particularly in regards to C4ISR, precision attack, and the area of sustainability.

- That the use of contracturization by individual states and by the EU and NATO be more actively considered.

ENDNOTES

1. See Simon Duke, *The Elusive Quest for European Security: From EDC to CFSP*, Basingstoke: Macmillan Press Ltd, 2000.

2. Jacques Delors, "European integration and security," *Survival*, Vol. XXXIII, No. 2, March/April 1991, p. 100.

3. Tony Blair, "Doctrine of the International Community," Speech made to the Economic Club of Chicago, Hilton Hotel, Chicago, April 22, 1999, *http://www.fco.gov.uk/news/speechtext.asp?2316*.

4. See House of Commons Defense Committee, "Fourteenth Report: Lessons of Kosovo, Report and Proceedings," *HC.347*, session 1999-2000, London: The Stationery Office, 2000.

5. Lord Robertson, "European Defense: the Way Ahead," *Speech to the RIIA Conference*, October 7, 1999.

6. Right Honorable Chris Patten, "The EU"s Evolving Foreign Policy Dimension—the CESDP after Helsinki," Speech to a Joint Meeting of the European Parliament Foreign Affairs Committee with members of the NATO Parliamentary Assembly, 00/51, February 22, 2000.

7. Lord Robertson, "Opening Statement," Meeting of the North Atlantic Council, Budapest, Hungary, May 29, 2001.

8. Willem van Eekelen, "WEU on the way back to Brussels," speech given at Chatham House on September 22, 1992, p. 3, *WEU Press Review*, No. 161, September 24, 1992.

9. "The Strategic Defense Review," *Cm.3,999*, London, HMSO, 1998, p. 2.

10. "Statement on the Defense Estimates 1993—Defending Our Future," *Cm.2270*, London, HMSO, 1993, p. 10.

11. The role of the media in influencing public opinion has been clearly evident in Britain with the recent airlift of wounded from Bosnia. Operation IRMA, the British aerial evacuation of a number of seriously wounded individuals from Bosnia, was due largely to the media focus on the plight of one child.

12. See Adrian Treacher, "Europe as a Power Multiplier for French Security Policy: Strategic Consistency, Tactical Adaptation," *European Security*, Vol. 10, No. 1, Spring 2001, p. 33.

13. Britain had Commander-in-Chief Channel; and the Unitd States, Supreme Allied Commander Europe and Supreme Allied Commander Atlantic.

14. See Michael Clarke, "French and British Security: Mirror Images in a Globalized World," *International Affairs*, Vol. 76, No. 4, October 2000, pp. 725-739.

15. "London Declaration on a transformed North Atlantic Alliance," issued by the Heads of State and Government participating in the meeting of the North Atlantic Council, London, July 5-6, 1990.

16. "Rome Declaration on peace and cooperation," issued by the Heads of State and Government participating in the meeting of the North Atlantic Council in Rome, November 7-8, 1991, *Press Communiqué S-1 (91) 86*, November 8, 1991, pp. 1-8, p. 1.

17. The Alliance's strategic concept, agreed by the Heads of State and Government participating in the meeting of the North Atlantic Council in Rome, November 7-8, 1991, para. 25.

18. "Beginning of meeting of Defense Planning Committee—recommendations from Military Committee on new structures of forces and command," *Atlantic News*, No. 2,378, December 13, 1991, pp. 1-2, p. 2.

19. *Idem*.

20. "Defense Capabilities Initiative," NATO Press Release NAC-S(00)69, *www.nato.int/docu/pr/1999/p99s069e.htm*.

21. Luke Hill, "Rapid reaction HQ shortlist down to nine," *Jane's Defense Weekly*, January 31, 2001, p. 3.

22. Meeting of the WEU Council of Ministers, Paris, October 10, 1990, para. 3.

23. Meeting of the WEU Council of Ministers, Paris, *Communique*, December 10, 1990.

24. Treaty on European Union, Maastricht 1992, Article J.1, para. 2.

25. "WEU Council of Ministers Petersberg Declaration," Bonn, June 19, 1992, *www.weu.int/eng/documents.html*.

26. "The Amsterdam Treaty: A Comprehensive Guide—Common Foreign and Security Policy," *www.europa.eu.int/scaplus/leg/en/lvb/a19000.htm*.

27. Joint Declaration issued at the British-French Summit, St. Malo, France, December 3-4, 1998.

28. Joint Declaration of the British and French Governments on European Defense, Anglo-French Summit, London, November 25, 1999; "Moving Forward European Defense," MoD Press Release No.421/99, November 25, 1999.

29. Ministry of Defense, "Statement on the Estimates, 1999," *www.mod.uk/policy/wp99*, para. 17.

30. Right Honorable Chris Patten, "The Future of the European Security and Defense Policy (ESDP) and the role of the European Commission," Speech 99/215 at the Conference on the Development of a Common European Security and Defense Policy, Berlin, December 16, 1999.

31. Ministry of Defense, "Statement on the Estimates, 1999," *www/mod.uk/policy/wp99*, para. 17; see Michael Clarke, "French and British Security: Mirror Images in a Globalized World," *International Affairs*, Vol. 76, No. 4, 2000, pp. 725-739.

32. Right Honorable Chris Patten, "The EU's Evolving Foreign Policy Dimension—The CESDP after Helsinki."

33. *401X0078* Council Decision of January 22, 2001, setting up the Political and Security Committee.

34. Remarks as prepared for delivery by Secretary of Defense William S. Cohen, Informal NATO Defense Ministerial Meeting, Birmingham, United Kingdom, October 10, 2000.

35. 2308 Council-General Affairs/Defense: Military Capabilities Commitment Declaration, Press Release 13427/2/00, November 20, 2000, Brussels.

36. Right Honorable Chris Patten, "The Future of the European Security and Defense Policy (ESDP) and the Role of the European Commission," Speech 99/215 at the Conference on the Development of a Common European Security and Defense Policy.

37. *Idem*.

38. European Council Presidency Conclusions, Santa Maria Da Ferra, June 19-20, 2000.

39. Cologne European Council, Annex III—European Council Declaration on Strengthening the Common European Policy on Security and Defense, Press Release 150/99, June 3-4, 1999.

40. David S. Yost, "The NATO Capabilities Gap and the European Union," *Survival*, Vol. 42, No. 4, Winter 2000/1, p. 103.

41. International Institute for Strategic Studies (IISS), *The Military Balance, 2000-1*, Oxford: Oxford University Press, 2000, p. 297.

42. J. A. C. Lewis, "French Plan Bucks Trend in Defense Budgets Cuts," *Jane's Defense Weekly*, May 7, 1994, pp. 15-18.

43. See Andrew Dorman, "Crises and Reviews, 1945-2000," in Stuart Croft, Andrew Dorman, Wyn Rees and Matthew Uttley, eds., *Britain and Defense 1945-2000: A Policy Re-evaluation*, Harlow: Pearson, 2001.

44. Michael Clarke, "French and British Security: Mirror Images in a Globalized World," *International Affairs*, Vol. 76, No. 4, October 2000, p. 726.

45. Michael Evans, "A woman's place is not in the SAS," *The Times*, February 12, 2001.

46. George A. Bloch, "French Military Reform: Lessons for America"s Army?" Summer 2000, p. 37.

47. See Kerry Longhurst, "The reform of the German Armed Forces: Coming of Age?" *European Security*, Vol. 9, No. 4, Winter 2000, pp. 31-44.

48. Lieutenant-General Sir Michael Jackson, "KFOR: The Inside Story," *The RUSI Journal*, Vol. 145, No. 1, February 2000, p. 15.

49. 2308 Council—General Affairs/Defense: Military Capabilities Commitment Declaration, Press Release 13427/2/00, November 20, 2000, Brussels.

50. Stewart Penney, "Off Target," *Flight International*, July 3-9, 2001, p. 36.

51. "RAF's C-17 Deal Seen as Model to Meet Other Airlift Requirements," *Flight International*, May 1-7, 2001, p. 20.

52. Joris Janssen Lok, "Extended European Air Group Signs to Share Airlifters and Tankers," *Jane's Defense Weekly*, February 14, 2001, p. 3.

53. A. D. Baker III, "World Navies in Review," *Proceedings*, Vol. 127, No. 3, March 2001, p. 32.

54. Coulsdon, "Hane's Information Group," *Jane's Fighting Ships, 2000/2001*, 2000, pp. 471, 639.

55. "Launch of New Assault Ship Albion," *www.news.mod.uk/stories/2001/mar/010309a1.htm*.

56. Coulsdon, p. 355.

57. Baker, p. 44.

58. "Royal Marines Get New Armoured Carrier Able to Tackle The Toughest Terrain," MoD, June 27, 2001, *www.news.mod.uk/stories/2001/010627a1.htm*.

59. Outcome of Strategic Sealift (RoRo) and Alternative Landing Ship Logistics (ALSLS) Competition, October 26, 2000, *www.mod.uk/index.php3?page=2&nid=1059&view=776&cat0*.

60. "UK to Revamp Armored Vehicle Fleet," *International Defense Review*, April 2001, p. 3.

61. Michael Evans, "Army"s Leviathan Battle Tank to Get the Bullet," *The Times*, April 14, 2001, p. 15.

62. Richard Scott, "Coming Up from the Deep, in from the Cold," *Jane's Navy International*, Vol. 106, No. 3, April 2001, p. 29.

63. IISS, p. 49.

64. Richard Scott, "UK Lays Foundations for Tactical Tomahawk," *Jane's Defense Weekly*, April 18, 2001, p. 35.

65. Richard Scott, "French Navy Outlines Equipment Priorities," *Jane's Navy International*, July/August 2001, p. 4.

66. Gideon Rachman, "Is the Anglo-American Relationship Still Special?" *Washington Quarterly*, Spring 2001, pp. 8-9.

67. IISS, p. 49.

68. "European Partners Give SOSTAR-X the Go-ahead," *International Defense Review*, April 2001, p. 4.

69. David S. Yost, "The NATO Capabilities Gap and the European Union," *Survival*, Winter 2000/1, p. 99.

70. House of Commons Select Committee on Defense, "Fourteenth Report: Lessons of Kosovo," *HC.347*, London: The Stationery Office, 2000.

www.ingramcontent.com/pod-product-compliance
Lightning Source LLC
Chambersburg PA
CBHW081803280526
45789CB00008B/2972